SELECTED POEMS
MAHBOOB HASAN

Mahboob Hasan

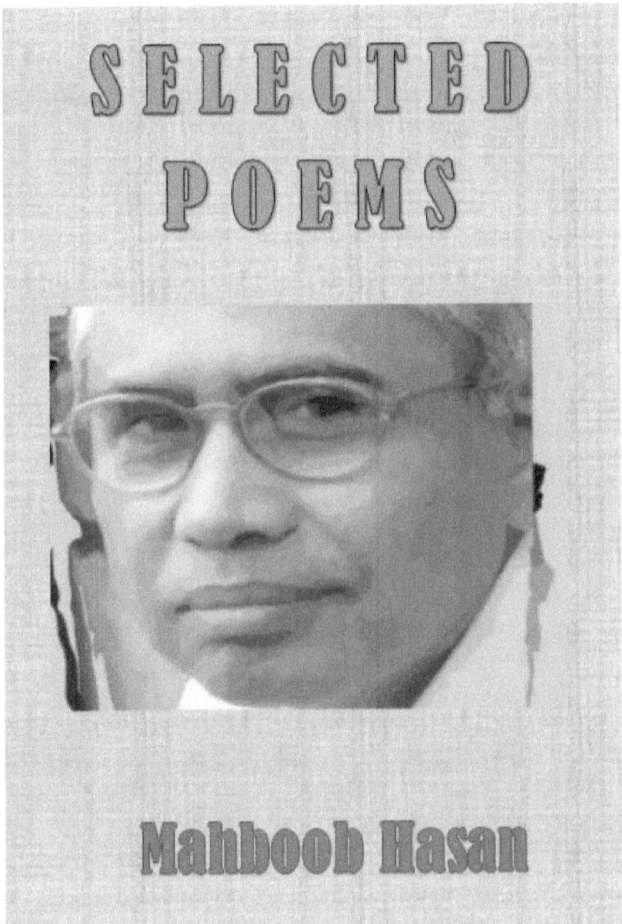

Selected Poems
By Mahboob Hasan
Translated from Bangla by Imran Khan

Copyright © 2018 Author
Translation Copywrite © 2018 Translator

This book is a part of Unobangal project
'Globalization of Bengali Literature' [Unobangal is a not-for-profit organization registered in USA]. On behalf of Unobangal Inc. this book is directly published in Amazon. No other publisher or intermediate agency is involved in publishing process.

All rights reserved. No part of this publication may be reproduced, distributed, stored in a retrieval system or transmitted in any form or by any means, including photocopying, recording, or other electronic or mechanical methods, without the prior written permission of Unobangal Inc. Only for book review purposes any part of the book can be quoted with appropriate reference.

Cover Design by Raghib Ahsan

Price: US$10.00 [or equivalent other currency]
ISBN: 9781728696690

Mahboob Hasan

Dedicated to
Poet Al Mahmud
The Soul of Bangladesh

INDEX

A

ALONE, 46
ANGELS ARE TAKING A SHOWER, 126
ARROGANCE, 39

B

BANDIT'S LOVE, 64
BARSHA, THE GIRL, 63
BEHULA THE REBEL, 82
BENDING THE THOUGHTS, 134
BIRD'S LIFE BIGINS, 55

C

COME BY THE OPEN WINDOW, RANU, 56
COME, THE TWO SUPERPOWERS, 28
COSMOS'S SALT, 44
CURRENT OF DEAD WORDS, 101

D

DAYS ARE GONE, 131
DEMONS AND ANGELS, 111
DO NOT PROVOKE ME, 133
DOES THE MOON DROWNS, 91

E

ENCHANTRESS, 129
ETERNITY PASSED UTTERING YOUR NAME, 59

F

FEAR, 107
FLYING POEM, 124
FOR MOTHER, 132
FOR YOU, 27, 41

H

HAY MOTHERLAND, 36
HER PROTECTIVE AMULET, 120
HIDE AND SEEK PATRIOTISM, 118
HILSHA FISH POLITICS, 128

I

I GAMBLE, 40
I ALWAYS, 104
I WILL WRITE NOTHING, 109
IN SLEEP IN WATER, 116
IN THE NAME OF HUMANITY, 47
IN WHATEVER THE NAME TO CALL, 58
INFAMY, 60
IS THE PEN A LIAR?, 119
IT'S TIME TO AWAKE, 125

L

LET'S HIDE THE TRUTH, 86
LIKE A CHEETAH, 87
LIKE REVELATIONS, 106
LOOTER, 100
LOVE'S PHRASE, 38

M

MOONLIGHT DIVES IN AFFAIR, 70
MUNAJAT/ PRAYER, 105
MY RIGHTS, 130

N

NATURE, 76
NAYANTARA, 49

O

OBLIVION, 30
ON BIRTHDAY, 122
OPEN THE DOORS OF HEART, 57
OUTSPOKEN 1, 65
OUTSPOKEN 3, 67
OUTSPOKEN 4, 68
OUTSPOKEN 5, 69
OUTSPOKEN 2, 66

P

PAST WIPES DOWN TEARS, 96
PICTURE OF A GREEN BENGAL, 81
POEMS FILLED WITH FOG, 127
Poems of Mahboob Hasan, 13
POLICE'S DEEDS, 112
PRESSED LIFE, 93
PUBLIC SAFETY LAW, 80

R

RAZOR SLASH, 43
RULER, 79

S

SATAN LICKS MY FACE, 135
SLEEPFAIRY KISSFAIRY, 110
SLEEPLESS CROWS AT NIGHT, 89
SOLITARY WINDOW, 61
SOUL OF MEMORY, 94
SOUL'S NARRATION, 62
STEALING YOUR EYESIGHT, 72
STILL ALIVE, 83
STORY OF A FEW FLOWERS, 34
STORY OF THE RIVER, 50
SUNLIGHT PLAYS AROUND, 117
SURPRISED, ONE DAY, 103
SURREALISM, 123

T

TELLING MYSELF TO BECOME RAIN, 98
THANKS TO THE POWER MINISTER, 92
THE ARGUMENTS, 85
THE WAIT, 35
THEY MAKE A LIVING SELLING BRAINS, 53
THIS ILLUSION WILL NEVER GO AWAY, 114
TO THE JOURNEY, 31
TRANSLATING NATURE, 37
TV AND DARKNESS, 52
TWENTY FIRST CENTURIES WILL, 77
TWO POETS, 71

U

UNDER THE BUTCHER'S BLADE, 42

W

WANT SOMETHING NEW, 88
WHAT IS RAIN, 102
WHAT IS SPORT TO THE CAT IS DEATH, 78
WHAT'S UPWITH HIM, WITH HER, 75
WHATEVER, 48
WHITE RICE, 90
WHO ARE YOU, 73
WORDS ARE SCAMPER, 115
WORLD SHINING IN SUNSHINE, 108
WOUNDED GOD, 29
WRIT CASE, 113

Y

YOUR ROOTS, 32

Poems of Mahboob Hasan

Syed Manzoorul Islam

[Translated by: Imran Khan]

Mahboob Hasan's poetry published twenty years back named Tondrar kole horin (Deer on Tandra's lap). This headline along with some words used in poems' headline such as roddur josna (Sunshine moonlight), haowa (wind) told us where he felt his debt was. A few of his poems struck me with lines like "kuyashakamuk du'ekta (a few fog-loving)/ dotala bari (two storied building)/ Jiaraffer moto uki mare(take a peep like Jiraff)" "palte jasse, palte jassi (changing everythings, changing I am)" or citol macher moto dhumur irshar dheu tole (waves of jealousy smiles like flatfish) then we realize he was deeply engaged with Jibonand Das, came back with some saving after his long journey, and added his words and fantasy with Mr Das' world. That made Mahboob Hasan a much-matured poet in his first poetry book. The word "Kuyashkaum" is his own creation, "Jiraffer Moto Uki mare" resembles Jibonanond Das' spirit. Both of these styles have enriched

Mahboob Hasan's poems. Each of his books have the same styles. In 2001 publisher Ayon Prokashoni released his first ever poetry collection combining his "Toamar Protik" (1986), "Nisorger noon" (1990), "Amar Akash"(1980), "Sopnogulo bikri hoye gese" (1999), "Nirjon Janala"(2000) and "Tini Kothok Silen"(2001) books. This collection of poetry represents his sense of debt and investment as we as his way of thinking and the way he sees things. This collection represents his growth as poet and getting to a place in poet society; his materials and skills, own and collected and repainting a fantasy world, allegory, anxiety is also represented continuously in these poems. His poems also published after 2001 but I still see him as I saw him in his book "Tini Kothok Silen". He was not very different from any published (in newspaper) or unpublished poems in this collection. He may have found some new ideas, experimented a little with symbolism, but he still is the same poem at heart published by Ayon Prakashoni years back.

Inside the collection he has been introduced as "Multidimensional poet of the 70s". the word multidimensional has been used so maney times in our country that now it has lost its depth. We don't want to use it to introduce Mahboob Hasan, instead let me give you the gist of it to understand why the term was used in the first place. Seventy's poets in broader stroke have always gave importance to our country's beauty, history, lifestyle and the ruthless truth behind national and international politics. May be a poet who comes from a country that freed itself by sacrificing lives in brutal armed combat always takes the side of those in any society who are ruled by colonial suppression, occupier governance and are divided through racism. It was so normal for seventy's poets to take a stand internationally recognized. Mahboob Hasan's poets definitely ads a layer to this international stand of seventy's poems. If we want to find more about his poems then we need to see their construction, language and overall tone with meaning. Needless to say Ayon Prakashoni's collection made it easier.

Besides Jibonanond Das, Tondar kole horin, introduces us with Mahboob's another mentor, Al Mahmud. The poem "Ekjon cashir golpo (A farmer's tale)" makes an Al Mahmud like impression. We also find Al Mahmud's influence directly and indirectly in other books. However, as a poet, this borrowing from others influenced and made Mahboob Hasan to construct his own ways of telling poems. His creation is his own, it is his signature. It does not have another people's shadow. He has written long poems, many of them are descriptive, meaning he expressed his experience and journeys. This kind of narration expands as we dive deep, then they deconstruct themselves and eventually take the reader to the center of the narrative.

Mahboob likes to talk about his childhood since he finds a massive gap between present times and his past, this gap is not just time gap, they are also emotional and uneasy. He likes to tell stories of cities where modernism, organized hair styles and trend work as smoking mirror to hide the decay of the society and concrete jungle sucks away people's roots. Narratives need structure to tell these stories. But only narration cannot be enough to make meaning out of poems. Poems have their own tone in their own world, they have mystery, and uncertainty and they become clear when Mahboob Hasan changes the tones, moods and path. He dives into an epiphany from his narration. A sudden bright idea, a matter of sensitivity, a lightning of feelings; a good thing about epiphany is it creates abolition, uses thick senses of origination. Somudrer kase amar shopno othoba josnar niche (my dreams are closer to the sea or under the moonlight) ellipses by using epiphany.

Love is a subject matter in Mahboob Hasan's poems, but it does not create any romanticism. He does not have many romantic poems. Mahboob is not interested taking Love as an only subject matter to explore. That is feelings like depression, wonder or sadness is found in his romantic poems. Or feeling unsettling like the unorganized ways of the big city is in his romantic poems.

Why so little of love-lyric in Mahboob's poems? Is this because he keeps busy to keep the ledger of life mistakes; suffered by civilization's decay; he looks for his roots and this exploration does not comfort him, because life here is crazy, he is afraid for civilization's existence threatened by super powers or he has been walking down life's path holding his sorrows.

He wants to tell stories of flowers, but his stories end with- "tikhno ekti citkare (a sharp scream)" in which "chinnvinno kore jege uthlo (bursts out rising)/ manashuer kormokander ekti sokal (a morning with people's everyday works), he wants to tell stories of moonlight but it ends with a blood washed man found under moonlight; he wants to tell about a night but that nights ends asking a bunch of questions: "ei nobo utthito bhorer alo (this risen new dawn)/ keno tobe fire ashe amader nosto mone (why they come back in our dirty minds)?/ pouche jay amader hridoy hridoye (travels to all our hearts)/ je prithibite tar odhikar, se prithibi aj bikkhubdh, biporjosto birodhi batase (his rightful world is angry, tormented by the enemy wind)". The known world is changed, it's very complicated inside our minds, civilization is walking towards the horizon of darkness, how can love to survive with innocence and deep happiness?

Since an essence of Jibonanond like every day sorrow is found in Mahboob's poems, they offer an escape from all of it through a surrealistic door. Maboob used reality like this in many of his poems- distorting the materials in scenarios;

making inconstancy by giving a color, words or scene more importance- they are unparallel to reality, so that readers can find themselves in dimensionless destiny after crossing the paths of known dimensions. "Roddur (Sunshine)" or "Khabo kingba khabo na (Will eat or will not)" represent the shadow of that surrealistic expression. This gets praise when his passion and deepness of thoughts take us to a place where our mundane scenario changes, melts away and we find our thoughts, anxiety, happiness all mixed and melted away from the traps of reality. In his first along with other poetry books, one this is big with Mahboob Hasan- he creates a reality parallel to particular time period and reality or rearranged alternative reality; this reality and surrealistic at the same time; to us, this is known and unknown both. We feel this surrealistic real scene-color-smell-touch in our nightmares. This is why it is not easy to understand Mahboob Hasan's poetry.

Later published first of five poetry collections has a distinct subject matter, construction and a tendency of making new phrases. Country and present times are expressed with passion- but time becomes harder as time passes. "Ek notun jati eseche prithibite (a new race has come on Earth)", he, tells us they are a mixed race in his "Tomar Protik (Your Symbol)" book. He made satire against military rulers and the ones used military to rule like Ershad. Actually, he protested against military rule in many of his poems. In "Nishorger noon (Cosmos' Salt)" he used black boots in many symbolic ways; "Jolpai ghera shohor (city surrounded by olives)" reminds us olive colored dresses (dead people) instead of peace; "Jhule thaka kalo boot josnar gaye (black boot hangs on moonlight)/ khotmot khotmot (stomping)/ tolpar chole (brawl happens)"; there are many hidden directions like this besides direct narration- in his other books where his stand against war, military rule is vivid but also features nuclear era's horror, ugly and loveless ruling in the entire world. "Nuclear" is a much-used word in Mahboob's poems. His poems feature many superpowers and their ruling, how they are destroying freedom and killing nature; worry about the anxiety and fear for future. After seeing all these he even thinks "prokitopokkhe manush vishon hingsro prani (Men are really violent)".

Many poems in "Nishorger Noon" are long, dialogue based, since humanity, time and freeing from danger etc. relevant to many other subjects; love is also featured, but jealousy comes with it. Mahboob's regular readers would know he loves jealousy as a subject matter. He sees jealousy in many ways- tries to understand this strange feeling. Nature is also important in Nishorger Noon. Cosmos is evanescent. We have sent cosmos out. Now we build things naming them cosmos, which are unnatural, we get trapped by cosmos. In a taken aback mid noon, moonshine washed midnight, autumn wind flows yet, everything is dry, mist everywhere- makes us remember that elite city.

"Amar Akash (My Sky)" introduces one more matter-poems. Nature finds shelter in this poetry book, but another shelter is created which is poem. "jantrik sovvotar bishom bagane (in a vast garden of mechanic civilization)/ bohukal por …aj (after ages…today)/shopnodroshta mone hoy (feels like a dreamer)". from poet to poems, from poems to poet artist, Mahboob's exploration is everywhere. Mainly in his book "Tini Kothok Silen (he was a story teller)" he discovers poetry in his village. His "dhan chara prem nei (no love without paddy)" tell us that he is farmer at heart. In this book nature and poetry touched at a center in one epiphany of feeling.

Before this his poems were like imagistic, sometimes a necklace with many small parts of scenario, sometimes lyrical and sometimes foursquare. The book "Nirjon Janal (Solitary Window)" features short poems, with short lines. To make impactful and statement, he made hints. Sometimes they are filled with imagery. In "Shopnogulo bikri hoye geche (Dreams are being sold)" there is a sonnet sequence, which reminds us the construction style of sonnets and gives us a tour inside our mind' worlds, which is vast like our hearts. Sonnets are feeling based, but there is sense of urgency in them- a man ruled by time can feel that always.

Mahboob Hasan has spent thirty years as a poet and he has crossed a long way of moving scenerios, walked down many locations of experience. But his journey is not just get from one point to another. He is in love with the path, not the destination; he is not interested to the destination. This path is not smooth; it can bring harm, just like it can bring joy of someone else's happiness. All these emotions make Mahboob Hasan's poetry[1].

---

[1] the write up was made during Mahboob Hasan's 50 years celebration collection at the beginning of 2004.

SELECTED POEMS

MAHBOOB HASAN

FOR YOU

Today is one of the last Sundays
of the twentieth century
pouring down by the gap of my fingers
just like the moments of Afghan guerillas
swept away with the smell
of gunfire, with the song of death,
yes, just like this, the lover
is waiting bowing to your presence.
Counting the courageous time's obelisk watch
spending the golden days
of my life, waiting for you;
yet you know that
West Asia or the whole worlds
water drop is hanging by a threat,
by the gentle affection for armaments, and
spreading the wings like bombers from city hall
one the breast of motherland by
the opposite wind.

Mahboob Hasan

COME, THE TWO SUPERPOWERS

Like the two Superpowers,
I want to come to a secret agreement with you
not in a big city,
not in a sound-controlled adorned house
sitting on a cold matt in my mundane room's floor
      sitting face to face
world's best printing mill's cryptic symbols
      without the stamp
with the wicked intentions of restricting worlds
nuclear weapons
we are, meaning you and me
      two psychic superpowers
signing a secret white paper
we want to stop the strategic war between us,
and want to hang those two secret documents
      in the deepest corners of our hearts
using no strings;
yes, only this way
      the conflict between you and my heart can be resolved.
Come; let us love each other,
like the two superpowers
on the top of the tree branch with the colors of armistice,
let's fly the Peace flag of the century.

WOUNDED GOD

Wounded God flies away breaking the Cabot
he may have beautifully crafted angel wings
may had
the bones for spells of Apocalypse
disguised as a wounded bunny
        the angel of light
        came down from the heavens
        with eyes wide closed,
and then
he strokes down mountains being trapped
        broke down old houses
        touched angel leafs
like this
took away
        news of all
        one wounded God.

OBLIVION

My childhood
seen through the window of my heart
as Promiscuous as rashly played soccer by teenage boys
as Shameless as temporary goalpost,
as the Flag of linesman.

My whole childhood was like
the Bakul garden by the Mosque,
the sound of Azaan
and the bewitched face of a boy.

Alas, I cannot recall those songs and tunes anymore,
from my childhood.

Mahboob Hasan

TO THE JOURNEY

Why would I need a dimension for my journeys?
blood in my veins play an echo
to run out in the wild
in the middle of low-lying
tree surrounded by villages
and I go back to my childhood, peeping through
strolling for a time, I ask, who broke all these?
why would I need a dimension for my journeys?

I make a new society, a new trend!

Mahboob Hasan

YOUR ROOTS

I leave
Like afoolish oppressed man
throwing away your colorful egos on the path,
I leave;

I leave
With a piece of your shining shadow of anxiety
stuck in your eye glasses,
I walk off;

I leave
All alone leaving behind
your ego-centric big beautiful teary eyes
I walk off;

I leave
Hoisting all my tiredness and exhaustion
and holding tight the Worlds spectacular storm on my chest,
I walk off;

I leave
To the land of catkin
leaving your bag full of egos behind

And I go back to path of unknown
Implanted in my knees,
Are, your roots.

Mahboob Hasan

STORY OF A FEW FLOWERS

A deer runs by the lake, in a song
from the coffin of moonlight, the pouring down of
Screwpine, Kathmollica flower bunch and
Hasnaheena flower's enchanting fragrance.
Before stepping out, the awaiting Teak garden
putting medicine and clothes in a handbag,
they come by the lakeside at midnight,
and got stuck between the enchanting fragrance of
the Screwpine, Kathmollica and Hasnaheena.
And all were enchanted by the smell of the bouquet of flowers
Rolled down after asking what's on,
      In the vast yard of nature.

Instantly, with the sharp scream
broke the morning of
Human's activity.

THE WAIT

The wait for the dark night, the girl
stands before me
her nose ring and necklace
smiles like paddy field;
still Her fragile eye sockets
get covered in sadness.

And her voice
neck-bone like a curved moon
like an anxious poor young girl
the lament of hunger of the Third World
is now imprisoned in the cage of her Hope.

The dark girl who stands there
I look into her,
bent by waiting
her "stone statue" hijacks my heart,
I can't I can't read those
awaited anxious hungry ravenous eyes
        I can't.
My such failure makes me naked before "The wait".

HAY MOTHERLAND

The shadow that follows you
you know her
The one watching over your front yard
who still has blood stains in his finger nails
you know him;
The ones who has occupied the open highway
you know them-
The girl who has turned the city's head with her shamelessness
and now pulling your doors continuously
you know her;
Yet my motherland
you do not know own self.

Mahboob Hasan

TRANSLATING NATURE

Translating nature inside me,

Nature has spread her dark long hair
and has spread her Jamdani body with the colors of her consciousness
I sit putting her on my lap
I translate nature's dark long hair with my own words
from the corner of her ear with the restlessness of young girls
as the young hairs
play hide and seek,
looting in laughter in the silent sea;
I love and adore her,
I take my shirt off and open up my thought bubble,
so that forever lasting nature girl with her eyes
          lay bare her deep mysterious
bravery voice
          in my eyes,
I translate her
but cannot really match her,
Yet people do these kinds of things.

Mahboob Hasan

LOVE'S PHRASE

Your heart is touched by olive
under this scorching noon sun
anklet smiles lying like a turtle
I want your flesh and bloody heart.

Your long stare
cuts stones cut my heart
the darkness of night laughed with intense eyes
I ought to write your love story?

ARROGANCE

Every bit of it is sin,
your kiss in my body, in my body hair
makes me arrogance;

Arrogance
you hold too much arrogance with your hands
so I tied you up with my heart.
All of it is sin
roses and soil
put them up with paint and brush,
in the secret retina
in your glasses
lovers face lights up
vulgar kiss on that face.

All of it is sin
devine and disgrace
life of cards.

Mahboob Hasan

I GAMBLE

My ruler with pealed eyes
looks into the veins of my brain
if I light up like gunfire,
He looks on and laughs
his teeth are as thin-sharp as a fork
he moves like a witch
I feel scared
citizens are scared
humanity lives under such butcher's blade.

I gamble
with the fashion of gambling, taking off my wrist watch
        I gamble with life bravely,

Fear crawls
heart jumps out,
I feel humanity jumps around
        like fish out of water under a bear claw,
Ruler's eyes in the veins of my brain,
disciplines me.

I gamble with my body and bravery,
Can I save myself?

FOR YOU

My desire for you
Was spread lighting the path
Autumn wind swept away
my downfall in your wrath.

Sighs of ages
has had Extended my heart-land
your deep cleaver eyes
cleaned up only my desire's dusts.
I weave a crest of darkness
in your eyes light of credence
colorful light lights up at dawn
and wins my heart.

Mahboob Hasan

UNDER THE BUTCHER'S BLADE

Under the butcher's blade
dangles the Bengal
yet you came back thirsty
you came back being war-inundated
from Lebanon, you came back to your homeland
surrounded by armaments.

Mahboob Hasan

RAZOR SLASH

A razor slashes in the deep of the greens
a bloody scene is born
squirrels disappear in thin air…

Oh squirrel
her brown-bluish eyes fill up with fear,
lonely time flips;

Sunlight flies in the air,
spread away like rice pie cake
blood wet with snowflakes;

As if people's scream inside mosquito net
in sand-blinded darkness of the evening,
tree bark falls on the
        bloodstained wind,
then stood before the sharpened razor blade
as time stops forever
after a ghastly genocide, to threshold of a shining day.

COSMOS'S SALT

Termite eats away Cosmo's salt
woodland laughs
falls stale on the path
Drakes scavenge and eat
those rice-dust fragments,
        Broken winged,
Wingless penguin in water,
crocodile flaps its wings
these agitates simple minded people

Water cord dives into rice paddy
lonely noon bursts in laughter seeing that
fishes swim away under the boat
        Gets attacked
Fisherman's attack
has the stars ruling been burned by the sun?

battlefield calls the haunted house
        in all nerves
Cosmos's salt blasts away
bitter, tasteless
Gorgeous darkness of the noon
look there, over water
fish heads

flapping all over,
starts brings arrows of strong sharp palate.

Termites live eating the Cosmos's salt
nature's sister pokes these.

Mahboob Hasan

ALONE

To live away from the shinnig light of civilization
I will blatantly go back to village
where nature has spread vast greenery, and
paying off the debt of humanity
                bountifully;
To keep safe from civilization's fearsome anger,
I will hold tight a part of land
I will hide it in the deepest corner of my heart with love and brave affection
I will light up my own eyes with all the love
to cast away darkness,
the anger of civilization may not touch my land;
I will fight like a wild bull, alone.

IN THE NAME OF HUMANITY

Even Before Jesus stepped foot on Earth
the history of cruelty on human
in the name of humanity existed
but traditional men
don't know any of this history.

Listen to you, new-born,
to the history of your ancestors,
even if it feels nonsensical like a jungle
and like a melted century
in fact
Humans are quite vicious
the nature of human teeth, face and brain has made
their mark on nature, society and science.

Mahboob Hasan

WHATEVER

To blast the nicely melted sharp shinning sunlight's shade of your poems

fart yourself hard

with that much depth

within 24 hours You'll find those soft poems by the harsh sunlight-shadow

have become magic lamp

Feed yourself with bread and sunlight

or eat or chew a hotdog

eat like a carnivore

You'll see, the Earth is moving around the Sun or the Sun around the Earth

if you don't believe this

see the rising sun is threatened by bold blue clouds

even If you don't believe this

then think whatever you want to

only thing is, catch a nucleus

nothing remains

strong belief or not believing,

Whatever.

Mahboob Hasan

NAYANTARA

Nayantara Nayantara, in Nayantara flowers
starts of whose eyes, are you? Shores of whose eyes
you've blossomed absolute truth on the graveyard
you are a garden for the dead, never found such beauty on Earth
Bluebell vine never had such memory of woodland

Some people drink these words like The Quran's
verses under the moonlit night.

Nayantara Nayantara, whose daughter are you?
You've blossomed absolute love on the graveyard!
in your frame of beautiful memories hang the poems of crumbling soil
Nayantara, you are my absolute metaphor!

Mahboob Hasan

STORY OF THE RIVER

At the end of beauty and river
Sand bed
Thirst for water peeps
hope rises inside
wet water points to
Sand bed!
As beauty and river stops their excuses
blind night comes to an end
in the hearts of all folks, thirst for water
raids with an unknowing outburst!
Beauty is like river
fast like a woman's heart
                fleet of fainting sand
                thirsty for giant waves
The Padma loses her beauty
glorious beauty on both of her shores!
same as
other rivers!
Padma gets, if water gets in!
Red hedge sand bed will sink in the Ganges terror!
with the same fright
thirst flows
Some people burry them in history
at the shore

Sand bed of red hedge, laughs.

Mahboob Hasan

TV AND DARKNESS

TV and fresh fish
both know how to enchant
like a woman;
So long humans have bet their lives
by relying on fresh fish
and brought back on the shore by sticking them with the passion of hunger,
rice thin flock of fish;

Today they bring TV and
darkness as hard work's pay.

Mahboob Hasan

THEY MAKE A LIVING SELLING BRAINS

Making a living selling career's brain
making a living selling
sense of life
Brainless and senseless of a man, I am
living for ages in this city!
carrying headless corpse, countless
shocking number of mindless
corpses are found in here,
living here with them, in honor and in insults!

Corpses love loneliness
they attend to funerals with
duck meat regularly
wash hands
 wipe faces with fragranced handkerchief
Since their hearts move formless
they use peace
as their lover
Because their thoughts on
peace is roundish like hunger!
Hunger,
formless human's most important feelings
hence, they cut off their heads and senses in
Hunger's Kingdom

Mahboob Hasan

they fly the flag
                    of delicacy and
                        with bare backs
spend a solitary life
                            and build
monuments of peace.

Mahboob Hasan

BIRD'S LIFE BIGINS

Before my bird life began
        I heard you cry!
washing myself in 52's agony, I rose up in54
        as if Adonis was born piercing throw
the soil
                or maybe I was that tree's
child
                a new farmer of this fertile
land

From dusk till dawn I weave sharp sound-bunch
        and stars light up at night
        rice grew in my paddy field
I am the father-mother-son-daughter or great grandfather for a thousand years of that grain;
That first man
who thought of creating
Human life
I blasted away barbarian's ear holes with my first screams!

My poet life started two years prior of my own life!
In the soil of motherland, I heard the sound of agony!
This is how a bird life's murderer time passes.

COME BY THE OPEN WINDOW, RANU

I know
your life is secured
Twelve Franc sky and Fifteen Pound wind
is allocated for you, everyday
yet, Dhanshiri River washes your body
like serene Jibonanondo, sharp chisickcall of wagtail flows in your ear
sometimes you sleep touching dropped feather
sometimes your heart sings like a Tailorbird
and lands on Bengali soil!
You are a girl of Bengali poems
your married life is jailed in Western fragrance!

Come by the open window, Ranu
I will fall on you as gold dust
if you follow the history of generations
know that Adonis will be born
or one Heracles one day
in some sand bed of this Bengal!!

Mahboob Hasan

OPEN THE DOORS OF HEART

Many times

knocked on

your heart

Open openopen your

veiled heartland

open the door on the coast of your heart, let me park my love boat

Shaptodinga

In my honeycomb

Ihave floated procession of dinghies

held the sail, held the helm

for an unknown nation's unknown Princess's love web

bound my inside

so I left behind

Motherland;

Yet your doors are closed!

Open openopen up heart's doors woman

are you that memorable silver moon or a rider of love?

IN WHATEVER THE NAME TO CALL

Many times
I call you with your nickname
RanuRanuRanu
engraved the name Rini inside
as if Draupadi instead of an Angel
RiniRiniRini
in whatever name to call you
you always response
and if your ears can't hear the name
Ranu or Rini
Whoever is whose lust
eating soul's lollipop in the wind of wealth
floats love's Shaptadinga!

ETERNITY PASSED UTTERING YOUR NAME

Uttering your name has made it decayed
I remember your face like the decayed moon
I remember- these sayings went old
hundreds of thousands of years!
Erasing the picture of your name for the time being
new woman's face I frame, put it on my chest
she scratches in a strangely attacked fever!

Mahboob Hasan

INFAMY

The nights
made a mountain
of infamy
like a slaughterhouse Empress
I bring infamy every day from your mountain!

Mahboob Hasan

SOLITARY WINDOW

Can't understand the language
gestures or words
what does he want?
Let the window of heart keep open
feels Like the rough skin of grasshopper
demands
are kept
in love's proteins!
a solitary window of noon!

Mahboob Hasan

SOUL'S NARRATION

At twelve fifty nine
I can stop the pen inside me
Does your soul live in sea of soul?

Your demands are like colorful
clothes and shoes, seeing your nature
feels like this isn't your occupancy right's heartland
she isn't the fertile paddy
field named Solitary
or any girl
in a formless noon, for whom
you are lost in love in the afternoon
who lives in this world hungry like me?

BARSHA, THE GIRL

Girl named Barsha, pierces my soul with spear
greens become house-wife's heart, yearn like Radha
in heavy rain
blue sky plays tremendous sound of clouds
girl named Barsha, pierces my soul with spear, by
the flaws of her character!

Mahboob Hasan

BANDIT'S LOVE

A bandit has come as rainfall
Is rain a pirate?
Is he defined by sudden attacks?
Sudden attack bringing fear
terrorizing laugh of the pirate
my lover gets scared to death
she gets Goosebumps,
shivers is fear even in my chest's warmth!
The sky is an ocean of waters
Does the rain command the clouds?
I heard of my love in the music of rain!

OUTSPOKEN 1

An woodpecker bites my chest as your clothe flies on me
and I feel so happy
my injured-warmth feels like absolute love
painful
can never find a cure!

Your lips are such beauty
my greed for kissing them dives into
an abandoned ocean!

Mahboob Hasan

OUTSPOKEN 2

Lips are for kissing
then young lads sharpen their hacksaw like lips
by indulging lots of kissing

Their teeth glace at sunlight
with Chitkir brunch or with Mailat's fragrance
young lads brush their teeth.
Then a right to kiss a beauty is born!
But be careful young price!
From the poison of the teeth

Mahboob Hasan

OUTSPOKEN 3

Kissing is the biggest guesture of love
where can I find meaning?
as true as breast
Bengali cinema calls!

OUTSPOKEN 4

Only an insane understands pure love
which is why all the lovers of the world
are insane fools
abandoning all their business
run away from Bokhara, Samarkand
is this the greatness of love!

OUTSPOKEN 5

After leaving the kingdom for her cheek's mole
The lover wins the whole world
But a free life without any love
Is a hollow life!

Mahboob Hasan

MOONLIGHT DIVES IN AFFAIR

Today I've seen that the moonlight isn't a saint

After covering midnight, she
follows the southern wind
and the sleep selling poet.

Hunter police blows whistle
who goes there… who?
Dipped in that enchanting moonlight?
Moonlight doesn't care the police whistle
she walks by swinging her waist
as if she is a dark-skinned separation-
in the wide open of the midnight
Madhucaindica she is, floats
away with favored world

after her affairs moonlight comes down on the enchanted-intoxicated world!

Mahboob Hasan

TWO POETS

I am a five dimensional poet

I bloom as a pair of throne worn roses in fearsome anger!

In this dusty-Bengal

rice seedlings tremble in heavy wind where I live in harmony with the soil

that's me

spreading myself in every corner by the bay of wind in the entire truth;

                                        I am a seven dimensional poet

I am a green paddy farmer in the eyes of a startled Dove

leaving behind the aura of a warrior's life, I peep

as if Bengal's Tailorbird

that's me

spreading myself passing life as sunny as the sun by the bay of wind in the entire truth.

STEALING YOUR EYESIGHT

Don't you get it girl
love is a sharp sword!
by my hand;
shining light falls on my face
you are riding on love today
yet why don't you understand this?
Heavier than words
heart's thirst grows
looks at here and there!
Steals eyesight;
Stealing your eyesight
starts of my eyes!

Mahboob Hasan

WHO ARE YOU

Who you girl, holding on the backdoor, peeping through
your beauty is like ripe paddy field
gleaming like fire
will by yard catch on fiery blaze?
or am I surprised getting the eyes of anhalf-witted poet!

You got down from
a newly made boat
stepping softly with your colored feet
stood by the back-yard door

I was struck with astonishment
with the fiery beauty of the new farmer girl
which river plays in your wide eyes, girl?
Or is it a lake?
Has the woman's body come down from the afternoon?
What's her name? What's yours?
Ganges! You lust longs for decades
float your raft
let the new farmer's house be washed away!

RICE SCENTED RED WHEAT

Mahboob Hasan

Goodbye fish and meat cravings
in the dreams of White rice
lover's memories keep awake!

Rice scent for so many years
red wheat
thirst for Grilled and baked greens
               for an ardent desire
               a farmer only gets
foamed rice
In dreams without salt
habit of life
licks on own fingers!
And gets beaten in every night's dream
waving pincers hand
out of habit
in heavy rain…
White star-flowers mix with rice scent
night's sky is the witness
               Charles's Wain
Red wheat yellow thirst in farmers' hearts
for ages
the thirst remains
mud bound human lonely in this labyrinth…

Mahboob Hasan

WHAT'S UPWITH HIM, WITH HER

A cuckoo is calling
piukahapiukaha
What's up with him? with her?
Mayna's mother has eaten coal
        What does that mean?
Her love becomes grass!

A bird calls in a tired thirsty voice
lakes-rivers, canals-marshlands all have dries out ages ago!
Covering underbelly by sand bed the river lies like a raped woman
thirst grabble the water; people listen to the sound of waves
enchanting sound of Youth's bangles' flows through the ears of people
Mayna's mother has eaten coal
as if someone sharpens the knife
calling of cuckoo is thirsty
flies away somewhere else!

NATURE

Even in autumn it rains!
You have also changed
clothes shoes and other attire

My zoo of a home burns in fire!
              Home gets covered in
melted wax!
Autumn leaves falling spring so far
clad wife has come in her domestic life
in Incessant rain fall
memories of thousand years
clothes and attire
who changes?

Mahboob Hasan

TWENTY FIRST CENTURIES WILL ABSORB SLEEP

Sleep absorbs my eye's light!
                         Sleep swallows my minds
darken!
Bad times are coming through a super highway, lying sleepless on ocean surface
intoxicated Earth breaking the laws of politics spinning in outer space
selling stars in the deep of night and days in the rampage of money hungry monster
                         knocked out by blood pressure sleep absorbs mind's fire
sleep swallow's sleep's colors
twenty first century is rising like a Phoenix in the reflection of tough times!

Mahboob Hasan

WHAT IS SPORT TO THE CAT IS DEATH TO THE RAT

It rained heavily last night
in winter's start and during shivering cold
has jumped in every corner like a hungry tiger

were we ought to see this disaster?

Mahboob Hasan

RULER

After death, comes the doctor
I walk down in the heart of the village thinking this idiom.
People believe this idiom quite sincerely.
Only they do not follow it!

Mahboob Hasan

PUBLIC SAFETY LAW

You said halt; stay there!
Being surprised shocked me stood still.

You covered beauty with city
made stunning civil land!

Thick darkness every where
blood sucking bat
Flew away sucking on unsuspecting time
throwing the coir on you!

Like a Sinking ship's mast where did you hide
              Leaving me alone!

Mahboob Hasan

PICTURE OF A GREEN BENGAL

In a costive forest
thousands of women during commencement stands
topless!
With a sweet smile
flying the flag
of plague!
Monsters have surrounded the green-Bengal!

Mahboob Hasan

BEHULA THE REBEL

Shy souls, these lovers known as humans
or tow legged jealous animals who have survived
for millions of years
built civilization, brought the lights of
disillusionment
as if their hearts are moonlight-cleaned moons
painted the picture of Parvati as lover in their minds
or maybe saint woman Rabeya Bashri
Sita is good for cultivation, she
makes the nature green with her fertility!
Even the mothers of Gods and Giants
are women,
                    Is she love's beauty fornature
or is she Behula?
With her wrath broke the stores of punishment
Behula becomes the rebel
of Bengal's waves!

Mahboob Hasan

STILL ALIVE

Wanted to leave dancing but didn't
sunlight of Baishakh left, dust and
dirt, wind dances
on the leafs of trees
making the sunlight
dancing and winding with googly song
the shadow of Ramna park lake
left like ducks make gentle ripple effect;
She also left yesterday
dependence on the spinning of blood in Baishak's
fearsome storm did not started yet, -
I wanted to leave but didn't,
and so I'm alive? Untimely
love of trees, sunlight and rain
and so many other things
forced me to sit in a corner by grabbing my neck for
keeping me alive, -
didn't go to Ramna's Banyan's
roots, so life is very dangerous
As if Banyan roots are death's top
killer's star-land in deep eyes, -
heart's green family
will be destroyed;

Still living

and dancing, cannot be uttered anymore
a demon has come for a blood-bath!

THE ARGUMENTS

1.
All the arguments are pointing at you
what can you say about that?
if the days shine with vernal sunlight
why are the nights so dark?
Tell me Hasan,
Where did all these black come from?
2.
Who's got the guts
to avoid you?
Only you can!
3.
Only you can lay a trap of old wive's tale
because, in this beef loving society
you are the leader!
That is why the arguments are pointing all the finger at you!

LET'S HIDE THE TRUTH

Truth is hidden in never ending rackets

some can find, some cannot-

I never looked for it, truth itself comes to me like a shameless women,

and I feel alive

get the rhythm to run forward;

The way Shamol talks, it feels like talking big is his habit

and truth? That's Shamol himself-

I Can relate, I relate in soft-green and in truth-lies

and lies wares, even though the venom

is a forest of never ending thoughts, let the forest fire

consume the whole woodland

Why would your business still run?

LIKE A CHEETAH

The night falls like a Cheetah
on your green face
saffron like light extinguishes, like twilight-
you slowly roll on the side
you are Earth's daughter
               Twenty first century

Cat's relaxed crafty steps in the whole forest
you pour your heart
in the greens of the grass
scent of lime, nonchalance!
time!

Mahboob Hasan

WANT SOMETHING NEW

After finding many analogies and symbols between my cornea and starts in the sky

in many poems

        at noon or afternoon, at lonely midnight

illusion by Jibonanondo's strange wonders

                              we swallowed!

Now there isn't any loneliness with the starts of my eyes

they are always busy with the epidemic of speeches and statements-

and public awareness pops like drums

as if big palm got ripe in early autumn's sun

restless time plays in the face of popular politician.

Analogies and symbols are now owned by politics!

SLEEPLESS CROWS AT NIGHT

Electric city awakes under moonlight, blind night
crows rise at twelve at midnight
moonlight plain in the calling of crows Ka-ka-ka
memories jump around
spring is transparent like crow's eyes, like a clear night washed in moonlight
crow's ka-ka doesn't sound harsh anymore
old crows' whispers bubble at black night
ransack like moonlight
or it's good to say that
crows enjoy more freedom than men
and crows enjoy freedom-
men cannot; only dream
to roam around in the fantasy world like moonlight
men cannot recognize if their rock like conscious
can float or drawn in water!

Mahboob Hasan

WHITE RICE

White rice
like Nyctanthes smiles the gloom of dawn!

They cannot smell the scent of Nyctanthes
only the smell of rice
enchants them, always!
Termite gets the right to aggressive hunger!

They know nothing; of this land's,
of soil's fluttering taste-
They know that the soil; clay made human and that unending blue sky
is deep like fate!
The moon knows that stars are drawn by the moonlight; the old women
on the moon named Caderburi
spins the spinning wheel
Dreaming about in the light of hostile life
foamy white rice
granary full of paddy, corn bin and parched rice
                their thoughts
plays in the store of dreams!

Mahboob Hasan

DOES THE MOON DROWNS

The moon comes down into me
Dives in
I drown in her water
Coming to drink water,
who drowns the moon or me!
Salty wind in the ocean of sunshine
Sinful time's missile carrying
warships guard blurry moonlight
Will the moon drown!
In the milking minds of pretty
women, moon drowns
Thinking of the White twelve
year old girl at midnight deep inside me
I get hurt every time
Crossing autumn's swinging
paddy field City-Baul!

Mahboob Hasan

THANKS TO THE POWER MINISTER

Thanks to the power minister
A big shiny moon rose last night
blasting the electric poles
          night washed in moonlight puts a
smile in the face of the city
Did anyone see fox's taken aback steps
or the moon's smile

As the unwary citizen scold at the minister
moonlight disappeared
moon followed it;
Worn-out men lingers around past memories
memories eat up molasses made sweeten, with the
crunchy taste of sweets made of nuts
people come back home
Moon visits Dhaka as a tourist passing the dark hole
          on the request of white path!

Mahboob Hasan

PRESSED LIFE

Darkness makes me jump
around in river water childhood
disciple, trapped as a fish, pressed and windy life
childhood plays in wavy water
smiles toothless
young times enjoys coconut
with ultimate satisfaction at noon
teals swallow youth, dust and dirt of conscience
heart dives into parched rice and milk, mind flies like cotton
flies in the rage of yarn
childhood still flies in
the rumbling wind of Baishakh
we pass the epidemic of diseases and plagues
but house-wife's hawk like eye follows
diseases spread away in the sky and through the air
childhood gets scared
ghost eats up sweets of belief;
Darkness makes me jump around in river water
a pressed life!

Mahboob Hasan

SOUL OF MEMORY

I make the highway naked
you are a black slave
in concrete
        Adam's face!

Shameless photographs
speaks up
highway gets naked everyday
complete fool!

Photographer's creative finger clicks the shutter
bleeding
black slave makes trembling noise
 with procession's slogan!

Known face floats out in the chemical tray from the yellow
as if flatfish's cremation in deep water!
and sister's, mother's, brother's bloody faces are
        covered in bruises
scream cries in every fold of
        wagtail's feather!

Making you nude everyday

does not fulfill the insatiable thirst for making you
naked, does not fulfill, does not…

Mahboob Hasan

PAST WIPES DOWN TEARS

When your faces are spread across
I cross the bridge of relationship
life left behind
past life-
Baishakh, Jaistha, Ashwar, Srabon rainfall
can there be a monsoon made of tears!
is rain the tears of Earth!

Men only have the hurry to flee on the inside
secretly or openly!
Who want to leave behind crafts
all farming rhymes they had
learned in their muddy family
the dancing lights of fireflies turns on and off
yet we want their flawless
blackness in the dark of night

When peoples' faces are spread
around, 71 jumps out
I stand face to face crossing the bridge of relationship
past life
and unobstructed days,
The world wipes down tear in Badra and Ashwin

Mahboob Hasan

kinsmen's faces get covered in winter's fog
and their hand marks!

TELLING MYSELF TO BECOME RAIN

Sparkly moon in the extreme of the sky
watching the moon torn clouds
get murdered!
I export my mind
in the straight path
as if slingshot is ready to hit
moon rises after power outage
in the black of civil night
the beauty of moon
blooms
when the extreme of the sky appears blue as hell-

Stars light up city nights like gems
                turn on and off
                turn off and on
                      like neon sign
stars' sparkling in water's moonlight goes on
entire night
like the cheeks of a child the extreme of the sky
                    moon and laugh
heart's desire will get rotten after the night ends
clouds and moonlight smear
chains my heart in
                the cage of chest

and ask it to become cloud and fall as rain
>in a moonlit night
>to myself!

Mahboob Hasan

LOOTER

Thought the door was light
nature appeared as green moonlight
You are not human beings
just seeds of lives
Eating all of the
light's door
Green nature is the forest resource
I got naked
As nature has put up its butt on your face
and you are biting on its meat and bones like dogs
fucking it with your dicks
putting in its hole!
Everywhere stinks after you came
sunshine became sticky!

Mahboob Hasan

CURRENT OF DEAD WORDS

Talking to my mind
mind is always open
all the bolts are open 24 hours
My mind licks on air, fragrance
you get in
come get in Baishakh in my heart

Let all kinds of talking cover you without any obstacle
you get in like a Baul
unworried night and day
I seat on the door to the south
I seat with the heart of my primate
come the southern door
come southwest, come sky, and wind
come destroying differences and
        life span
       come in the heart
       let us talk in hearts
       in the current of spoken
dead words.

WHAT IS RAIN

Rain is a dancing old lady
young man's transition book
Immortal Joishtha in Baishakh storm plow and yoke
showing off belly with the soil
Indian myna celebrates in rain water
spear like Sharp water drop pierces the soil's face
rain is a small girl
love doll of a surprised youth
necklace made of seven colors of seven colored blues
yet rain is like naked sensual humid air
can anyone recognize?

Mahboob Hasan

SURPRISED, ONE DAY

Astonished, surprised!
dawns;
Murderous intoxicated sunlight
pours down everywhere-
Blood runs- in the pages of
morning newspaper
laughter!
Laughter of power isn't that charming,
Laughter like a whole inexistence
pours down murderous restless
floats the newspaper away to hell-
They;
As if a fountain surrounds their blood thirsty conscious-
Surprised! Only human's. they are
senseless; in veins
bending the streams of blood flows in veins
blood's surprise!
        Will be won one day!

I ALWAYS

Really, I am always alone
my skin turned to ashes by the scorching sun
belly full of wisdom
of civilization
Leaving the belly and shaking her booty
Prithula walks by
in the motor car-
colored history is
painted in her saree
alone!

Mahboob Hasan

MUNAJAT/ PRAYER

Holding Sickle, hoe and axe in hand
carrying plow and yoke on the shoulder
with aworn out chest and a lean butt
wearing a lungi like a wrestler
standing in the doorsteps of a giant building
looking at the highest peak of the building-
Hey God, when will I get the paddy?

Mahboob Hasan

LIKE REVELATIONS

I came out of mother's womb
like revelation reveled

I'm a poet
the sound of my first cry
echoes in the mountains
sheds of trees in the Baishakh's heat
salty sweat comes out naked after the
rainfall;
fresh green wind
swings the bald calm tree branch!
ka-ka black crow
hundreds of millions of Red-sun time passes
          will be covered
in the darkness of fireball!

When drowsiness wares off for the desire of mango
      mom gets shoved like mammals!

FEAR

Fear
always, all the time

Firey religion
means-
sceared after
being
converted-
because
he could not
hide his scesnt
after changing his attire
is the scent
Hindu or Muslim?

Fear
hides
sceared by religion
all us
where would we hide?

Mahboob Hasan

WORLD SHINING IN SUNSHINE

Toxic air today
there goes the green in ting-ting Rickshaw
sunshine stuck in her rubbed glass of her spectacles
some have taken fragments
of her cornea by a sharp knife
her eyes are now meaningless frozen bosom!

Time winks
by flying away the dress of a young girl in the streets in lust
humans are formless
endless moon in their dreams!

Cloning goes on the in the dreams molding in endless moonlight
countless human children
bow to machines!

Humans don't die!
sotheir habit sucks away the wild taste of sunshine and air
killing goes on for blood!

Mahboob Hasan

I WILL WRITE NOTHING

I will write nothing anymore!
some have crushed pomises of the ritght to goods
eat when you hear the knock wake up when eating- write! write!
My doors are open for you directionless open field
conscious is like a silent colored cuckoo
Write! Write!

I won't write any name
the way she looks at me as if loneliness shakes in the shadow
wind flies me away!
Cutting the roots of belief becoming
a lonely man
I get stubborn like a child
to not to write anything
suddenly silence grasps me and takes my away grabbing my ass
like a terrorist at the hanger of disorder
mowing the words of prayer like a cow!
Standing in the mist of illiterate, she laughs so loud
water comes out from her blisters!

Yet, I won't write your name!

Mahboob Hasan

SLEEPFAIRY KISSFAIRY

With sleepy eyes I write Sleep fairy
Ink stares at Dark fairy
Ear has become white   Flute fairy

Moon burns in October sky   Moon fairy
After the cold winter come   Cold fairy
Stars smiles with snowy eyes   Snow fairy
Dewdrops sparkle in grass in the morning Dewdrop fairy
Bring me a blue fairy   Blue fairy

I touch these nude fairies in the reality of my dreams

Light come out at dawn with the fog as sleep breaks
I don't have any tears but only dewdrop
                       No sound of waves
                       No sound of stories
                       No fairies and angels
                Fairies are in long lost
past!

Making the cosmopolitan embarrassed I go around the garden
Of green fairies with the red and blue fairies
               And I write a world of jokes!

Mahboob Hasan

DEMONS AND ANGELS

That moon has amazed you
burnet purified gold to ashes
moon like a pearl necklace of the vast sky!
Who do you shed tears for?
You cannot look into my teary eyes;
greens never saw this trap coming!
Building by hand, your love bird started family
washing with moonlight!

Since then you are an Angel

        I am a Demon
playing hide and seek like day and night!

Mahboob Hasan

POLICE'S DEEDS

I created a world with a spell
painted a sun with sunlight
a sky with clouds
poured down making a hole with sunlight
and started to play on my back!

Till the police
Showed up!

Mahboob Hasan

WRIT CASE

Sleep is son of bitch
not knowing the time
sleep is stuck with my son.

.
Cut the word sleep and curve a pretty woman's face from it!
I will appeal a writ about this in high court!
Court does not sleep!
Because they are the honorable judges!

Mahboob Hasan

THIS ILLUSION WILL NEVER GO AWAY

This illusion will never go away
rain has got fever
her eyes are teary
or is it an illusion made by the cold and her running nose!
Is Rain scared?

Don't you know her?
Summer's little sister Rain
heavy fall that breaks the sultry
the big bang of stormy wind!
        She is glumly in shame
sitting on the top of horizon bowing her head
she is lonely like a good girl, -
Don't flash her away with the current of flood!

Mahboob Hasan

WORDS ARE SCAMPER

Words are flying away as if they are angel princesses
to catch them so many times at midnight, I guarded moonlight
words meaning tricked and left me like angel princesses many times!
Life is such!
life scamps as a habit like words
full of tricks like a magician
anklet of words
stunned!

Words have travelled far away
they have swum across seven seas and thirteen rivers to, Canada
by the force of the habit of scamps,
who wants to
submit to magician's tricks like a fake lover
anklet of words
are like mid noon
formless, silenced, knocked down moonlight!

IN SLEEP IN WATER

Swimming away in my sleep
a fish swims pass me
red-blue-yellow-black, she's got all kinds of colors
suddenly I became a fish!
diving in deep water by her side
fish-man and colored fish
dive in deep water
an amazing palace in sitting under water
What is that monster sank this palace under water?
Remember, the king's palace under the Kaptai lake water,
I go and see the fairy tale of kids in my sleep becoming a fish!

Mahboob Hasan

SUNLIGHT PLAYS AROUND

Sunlight plays on the back of the pony
in the morning?
Noon plays on the back of a donkey
anyone gets tricked?
Why does afternoon run around?
looks for a darkness smearing sight!
For which desire?
Love of the flowers and fruits hangs on the trees
spring brings calm anger of the sizzling summer
why does sunlight play on the pony in the morning?

Mahboob Hasan

HIDE AND SEEK PATRIOTISM

found you!
From Memories black dust of oblivion
some have given dicks in my hands
my though bubble have blasted away-
fragrance of memories dances at
night under white moonlight;
Got you
restlessness, fear and surprise
I win myself-
leaving behind lively times of childhood
Found you
taking off the blood stein
all warrior men,
using phrases
along with love
anger-racism- sorrow and patriotism
Got you
History!

Mahboob Hasan

IS THE PEN A LIAR?

Through the glass window,
I can hear the wall whispering
do wagtails sing or wren-drongos in autumn?
I looked through the glass windows
but could not find the other side!
My window is filled with Kadam flower leaf's
I see some tailor birds dancing
do they sing, I am a deaf!
My ears can reach what my eyes can see!
My eyes cannot see what my ears can hear!
                And I'm such a tough bugger
even stones give up!

Yesterday whatever I saw
whatever I heard
all lies, like police!
My pen, is the writer of those lies!

Mahboob Hasan

HER PROTECTIVE AMULET

I have sorted from constitution
sigh filled Bright rights
surrounded by black fonts as they
	got caught like colored Hilsha fish,
could not breath freedom till today!
I have taken my rights to speak up
tricking like a plagiarizer student
and that stolen asset
	I have hide in the deep of heart's
memory lanes
in the rebellion lakes, in brain's veins-
Any assassin or spy, armed troops
or fermented rice eating farmer, apprentice singer, cinema's hero
or heroine's lightning smile
cannot take it away!

This habit of poking
becomes art in public certificate exams!
All the idiotic government secretary and slaves
with fake wisdom invested to your lord
no matter how much sacrifice of your life and youth-
taking from all side, some eat away everything!

Oh Emperor human soul

Mahboob Hasan

your unsatisfied heart
has hidden anger in every layer
you are the protective amulet of that anger!

ON BIRTHDAY

Sleep

covers up words of poem

hot morning!

Scorching sun burns the fifteenth of Baishakh month!

Diamond piece burns like our diaries

under such sweaty sun

    I was born,-

in the middle of month, with squeaky habit

Sleep

covers up memories

weaves dreams, a world of moonlight!

Mahboob Hasan

SURREALISM

I put down my pair of corneas on the reading table

let the mind run like an engraved bull

Why is the mind lonely when we have two eyes to see? This question pokes me- no right answer! Corneas are gone!

Mind explores the city, the country

even explores that far away moon

alone

no shadow of any other

Who would you give this mind?

Mahboob Hasan

FLYING POEM

Dancing like flying paddy
where do you go?
Flying like puffed rice binny parched rice
you are ill-timed clouds of the sizzling summer!
In the emptiness of mind
                I travel in the land of tears like you.
Empty heart falls in loneliness
curious air balloon
as if in shameless eyes opens a fountain of laughter!

Flying like puffed rice binny parched rice
some have offered yoghurt, where are the Ghosh's'?
                Healthy cows in cowshed
drinking away milk canals inside the head!
Look at my flying boat, field filled with ripe paddy
cow cart makes noise in the unbent month
sea of dust flying away in the drunk mind
parched rice has been made in the pigeon field
where do you go sizzling summer flying dusty stair?
I write Bengali poems, prose about you sitting here!

Mahboob Hasan

IT'S TIME TO AWAKE

If you excess now
then I'll bring general Pinochet
if that does not silence you then I will call upon the corpse of Dayar
then Marx and at last Hitler!
Stop now you guys!

Who knows where your well-being lies?

Not you; I will make monuments of democracy's proud fighters-
whole India doesn't have this arrangement!
Then sing now, my song
Spanish folk song and Aleman Jazz!
Societies think of Beethoven, Bach and
Alim Abbas-
You forget.

We need to wake up from sleep
in the long basin of sand-bedded
Padma and lean of Brahmaputra river!

Mahboob Hasan

ANGELS ARE TAKING A SHOWER

Angels are taking a shower in the falls of rain
fishes play by under water
under mushrooms, they swim by!
They sell the smiles of rain drops
and let the fragrance flow in the wind
smokey smelling human eye balls
atares upon playing a two stringer
at the white feet of angelic women
with steadfast amazed eyes.

Rain falls with a synchronized tune; they spend the mid noon on grass carpet
you bloom in the garden of angels
Is a frog garden like the rain fall of rainy month?
Or is the warmth of men is hungry for green!

Mahboob Hasan

POEMS FILLED WITH FOG

When the foggy moonlight becomes cold
you open up the doors and windows,

let the foggy wind come in through the door!
As cold runs after you like a terror you climb up rich people's balcony-
the spring village isn't far from there
they are blind!

In the civilizaton of so much money and access they filled their yards and beds with unneccessary things
and still left to have lunch at Eiffel tower;
and rest at night! that is no more, day and night 24 hours is the sound of money!
They own sunshine. Us suffering from
cold belong to this world!

Mahboob Hasan

HILSHA FISH POLITICS

Dhaka's streets are flooded with Hilsha fish politics!
The whole city searches in my chest pocket
as they dreamt!
I bring Hilsha scent upon opening layer of papers
and put on the pages of history
fresh scent
everything else is hoax!

ENCHANTRESS

Hope the enchantress
necklace of fine yarn
holding on with my breath everyday
this play goes on at the office with happy thoughts
at any moment my hope paper may tear apart
like this every moment passes by
standard flag
heart is scared, grab on to curiosity
as that kitten
healthy and fat in the pellet of hope along with nose
or showing red reddish whoever are winning
people's hearts everyday
I beg of them
betting on life
I keep hopes in dreams
Enchantress remains far, away

You are untouched forever!

MY RIGHTS

You are formless;
are that why magic amazes you!
I want magic spell with all I have;
with life's grinding machine
putting on two powerful unbreakable wings
I am not a son of Daedalus; not a great hero either!
My brain works faster than the horse
of Helios, you know that.
My wishes have no form; -formless they are-
Earth's marine, ocean and atmosphere
in my rights,
because, I am human!

Mahboob Hasan

DAYS ARE GONE

Many days have passed useless
days and nights of life went Unfruitful
darkness has spread fear
times at towns remain frightened
who are pulling on life's rope making unlawful intimidation?
Who are those villainous speech?
who are illustrious misadventures?

Whose black hand is on "Their" back,
why the roof of power went to others?
should a midget fall for the moon?
is power flashing? People want freedom!
Many days are spent,
like loose changes of dunks
good times clang on
unflinching me hang on the branches of those vocabulary;
just like clerks hang on buses daily
the city still wants to bit knowing about the underworld beneath the water
honey sellers lick cleans the juice of profit
like crazy!

Mahboob Hasan

FOR MOTHER

I went out searching for mother in autumn's dawn
not too far sunshine sits spreading
her legs floating pink layer –
I follow that path and open
my ears to listen to
mother's voice.
Hasn't my ear filled with mother's voice?
Hasn't my heart filled with her
melodious tunes of
Holy Quran's verse?
My conscious is filled with
her charm, her sweet words
and affectionate love melts my heart.

As I walk I see mango trees
have new buds on branches
with their colors, and smell I can see
my mother's face well.

Mahboob Hasan

DO NOT PROVOKE ME

Do not provoke me to tell lies
at least in this Ramadan!
Rain's scent is soft cold in late summer
truth is filled in that scent.

Who have been poking me to trade lies often
who have been blowing in my heart
making temptation
I have been swinging on the branches of
multidimensional reciprocity
wren drongo's black tail shines in the sky
sharp blade's lightning-spear
this hot wind will ware off by
peaceful chilling rainfall.
Do you know a looter slum?
named Rainfall in Dhaka
has risen its head with pride?

Don't provoke me to tell lies, God
only the Devil provokes to eat the forbidden fruit!

Mahboob Hasan

BENDING THE THOUGHTS

Thoughts are bending like roads
and streets in my dreams!
Is this called living in a dream?
Or has a dream came into
reality like they happen in stories-
I see our dreams becoming fairytales
taking upon the sword of heroes'
prince son of Kotal starts victory march!
our sons never get that sword of justice.
Rising its head high, Injustice has occupied the
bragging rights of the sky!

Thoughts are getting bend and broken, its scream
travels far, very far and not so far-
our festivals do not commemorate the stories of
kings queens prince and princesses
the ones who have suffered in sickness so long
they are happy today.

As if Hugo Savage has risen in Bangla!

Mahboob Hasan

SATAN LICKS MY FACE

A dark night like Satan
shivering in fear I wait for you
Adhara are you coming today?

Suddenly someone grasps onto me.
Can't see the face in the dark.
Soft fire straps me hard-
I am rising being purified by
your mysterious black fire.

Are you a mysterious woman flooded by
moonshine?
A foreign-girl,
or a wingless angel?
Who are you beautiful? Consumes me in darkness?
I shower myself in soft light!
I can't wake up in hundreds of years
Sunshine doesn't cast shadow; doesn't have forms,
silent darkness everywhere
playing affectionately
where would I go swimming,
at this treacherous time?

Woman like Satan licks on my
lips with sweet kisses!

Mahboob Hasan

www.ingramcontent.com/pod-product-compliance
Lightning Source LLC
Chambersburg PA
CBHW031423210526
45464CB00005B/2021